Design & Make
Pop-Up-Cards
for
Every Occasion

Adrienne Dawes

INTRODUCTION

Most children will have enjoyed looking at pop-up books. Cards and books which pop-up or move hold a fascination for children of all ages, the fascination lies in how the 'pop-ups' pop-up! Paper and card are about the most versatile and familiar materials we have in schools and by introducing children to several basic cuts they can create cards and books that come alive. Card Engineering as a means of teaching Design Technology therefore harnesses enthusiasm and enables work of a high quality to be produced. No matter what experiences of cutting and shaping card and paper the pupils have, the challenge of creating a three dimensional picture is an exciting and rewarding use of their skills. Opportunities to make pop-up cards and books occur many times throughout the school year, which provides children with a real purpose for their work. Once the basic skills have been introduced, then the pupils own creativity can be left to flourish. When the basic techniques have been introduced to the pupils and they have been given time to experiment with a range of materials, then the teacher must ensure that:

•The project / task given to the pupils is demanding enough to allow them to perform at a higher level.

•The task is interesting so that the pupils are encouraged to persist.

•A variety of equipment is available to ensure appropriate choices can be made.

•All equipment and materials are available in the class and they are easily accessible so as to ensure pupils make the correct decisions.

•Sufficient time is allowed to enable thorough experimentation by individuals, that they can practice newly acquired skills, be taught how to correctly use any new pieces of equipment, develop ideas and apply finishing techniques.

•The teacher needs to have the skills and knowledge necessary to intervene when appropriate. Experimentation and choice on the part of the pupil is very important. This book contains photocopiable resources and teacher / pupil instructions which will enable you to teach and practice a variety of skills and techniques appropriate to the making of pop-up cards and books. The activities are designed to assist adults when introducing new techniques to Key Stage 1 and Key Stage 2 pupils and when used by a whole school will ensure progression. The activities are intended to be used as an introduction and when the pupils have completed these introductory activities they should be provided with a range of materials and equipment to enable them to create their own pop-up on a given theme.

Cont

Teacher Preparatic

Copyright © 1996 Adrienne Dawes
Illustrated by Adrienne Dawes and Paul Sealey
Printed in Great Britain for "Topical Resources", Publishers of Educational Materials, P.O.Box 329, Broughton, Preston. PR3 5LT
(Tel/Fax 01772 863158)
by T. Snape & Co. Ltd., Boltons Court, Preston.
Cover Design: Paul Sealey Illustration and Design.
First Published April 1996. Reprinted September 1997.
ISBN 1 872977 24 3

TEACHER PREPARATION

The techniques needed to create the cards can be taught to groups or individual pupils depending upon their age and previous experience. You will need to know the children's experience level in the following skills and practice if necessary: Cutting, measuring, folding, scoring, tearing, finishing and sticking.

Pupils need to be made aware of the properties of a wide variety of sheet materials e.g tissue paper, sugar paper, plastics, newsprint, card - of varying thicknesses etc.

It is important that pupils experiment with materials before being expected to produce an iitem of 'quality.' They need to fold, tear, colour, cut and join to allow movement as well as stick and measure.

Folding.

Let the pupils practice folding sheet materials to see which will stand to assess the suitability for making a card. When appropriate the pupils need to be taught the correct way to fold:

i)   On a clear table
ii) Corner to corner
iii) Running clean fingers down the fold to press it firmly in place
iv) Scoring should also be taught [score using a spent biro or a pointed lolly stick]
v)   Measuring in cm and mm to fold a card in the middle or 3 ways - concertina fashion.

Tearing

The pupils should experiment with tearing in strips and also tearing shapes. Sometimes a softer, more appealing edge can be obtained with a softer torn edge rather than a hard cut line.

Colouring

The pupils need to experiment with a wide range of mediums for colouring e.g. felt pens, coloured pencils, paint and a variety of brushes, crayons, pastels etc. Children should question which ones are the most suitable for detailed work.

Cutting

A variety of cutting tools should be introduced to the pupils as and when appropriate for the individuals development and need. Scissors, right and left handed should be available as well as round and pointed ended. Safety snips should be available for cutting thick card and lolly sticks. Be aware of the safety aspects of all these tools as they contain sharp blades. Other examples include craft knives, rotary cutters, circle cutters, wavy cutters and perforators.

Join to allow movement

The pupils should experiment with joining card using a variety of materials that will allow movement e.g. string, pipe cleaners, brass fasteners, paper clips and treasury tags.

Sticking

There are a wide variety of glues available, some are more suitable than others for the card engineering work. P.V.A. is a strong glue which works well with paper yet can be messy and takes time to dry. Glue sticks are the most effective as they dry almost immediately and can be used for fine detailed work.

Measuring

Although initially measuring is not of great importance to the completion of successful 'pop-up' cards, later and when the pupils gain greater confidence and are introduced to more complicated techniques the pupils will need to use standard measurements.

During the activities the pupils will be involved in:-
•Observing
•Evaluating - an ongoing process which will involve investigating and disassembling simple teacher made and manufactured items.
•Exploring and Investigating - the pupils should choose materials investigating their properties e.g colour, strength flexibility etc., and relate these to the suitability of the materials for the making task.
•Organising and planning - resources need to be organised to allow pupils to select for themselves.
•Testing - could it work / look better? Does it do what was intended? What do others think about it?
•Explaining and communicating - the pupils should be encouraged to talk as a means of recording what they have done or are intending to do.
•Designing and Making - this book contains photocopiable sheets to enable new skills to be introduced which can then be developed and practiced in a variety of situations in the primary school. At a later stage the pupils should be provided with a range of materials and tools to enable them to develop the skill further. They should be allowed time to develop and refine the introduced technique and be taught the importance of quality.

All of these skills are applicable for any pupil at any age or level. It is the teacher's expectations, the materials, the resources provided and the development of the initial technique that will vary from stage to stage so that continuity and progression will be achieved.

Card Engineering skills for
KEY STAGE 1

Folded Pop-Up A simple no cut pop - up technique formed on the edge of a piece of card. Fold the card in half and fold the corner into a triangular shape. Whatever is to pop - up should be attached to the inwards folding triangle.

Rocking Card The pupils should be given a teacher prepared circle and when the circle is folded in half a moving - rocking card base is achieved. Effective decoration can be achieved by pupil drawn pictures or by sticking on characters / shapes cut from a collection of old / recycled greetings cards.

Spiral Cut Young children should be provided with a circle with the decreasing line drawn on it so that they can practice cutting along a pre-drawn line. The spiral shape is opened and closed when the cut inner and outer points are attached to the front and back of a folded card.

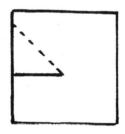

One Cut Pop-Up This cut can be introduced to groups or individuals depending on the pupils age and prior experience. No measuring is necessary and the pupils need only cut one straight line on the folded side. For very young children a drawn line will ensure a certain degree of accuracy. Fold from the end of the cut to the folded edge of the card forming a triangular shape. This fold needs to be pressed in well to ensure the success of the pop - up.

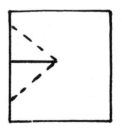

One Cut Pop-Up with 2 folds Fold the card in half and near the centre of the folded side cut a straight line approx. 3 cm long. Fold from the end of the cut upwards and downwards to the folded edge. These folds need to be pressed in well, folding forwards and backwards on the fold line approximately 10 times will ensure the success of the pop - up.

Curved Line Cut With young children a drawn curve will help to create a successful pop - up. From the end of the cut curved line, fold the card to the centre fold, press the fold in well.

Parallel Cuts This is a very versatile technique. Fold the card in half and on the folded side cut 2 parallel straight lines of equal length. It does not matter how long the cuts are but they must not be longer than half the width of the front cover of the card. Fold the cuts backwards and forwards 10 times and the pop - up will work correctly.

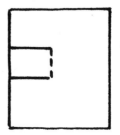

Jumping Frog Card

Technique used:
> Folded pop - up.

Equipment needed.
> scissors
> card
> felt pens and crayons

How to make the example:

Step 1. Photocopy the sheet opposite onto card or stick onto card, one per child.
Step 2. Photocopy the frog picture at the bottom of this page, one per child or use as a template
Step 3. Fold down the centre dotted line and then fold along the dotted lines to create the triangle. Fold the triangle in and out about 10 times finally leaving the shape inside the card.
Step 4. Cut out the frog shape and decorate.
Step 5. Stick the frog onto the pop - up triangle on the card.
Step 6. Decorate the rest of the inside of the card.
Step 7. Back the card and decorate the front cover.

How the idea may be developed.

There are many manufactured cards and books which use this simple no cut pop - up technique. Collect some books which demonstrate this method and let the pupils create their own after having investigated and practiced the technique.

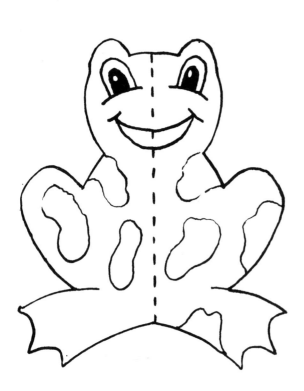

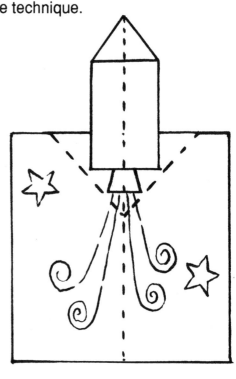

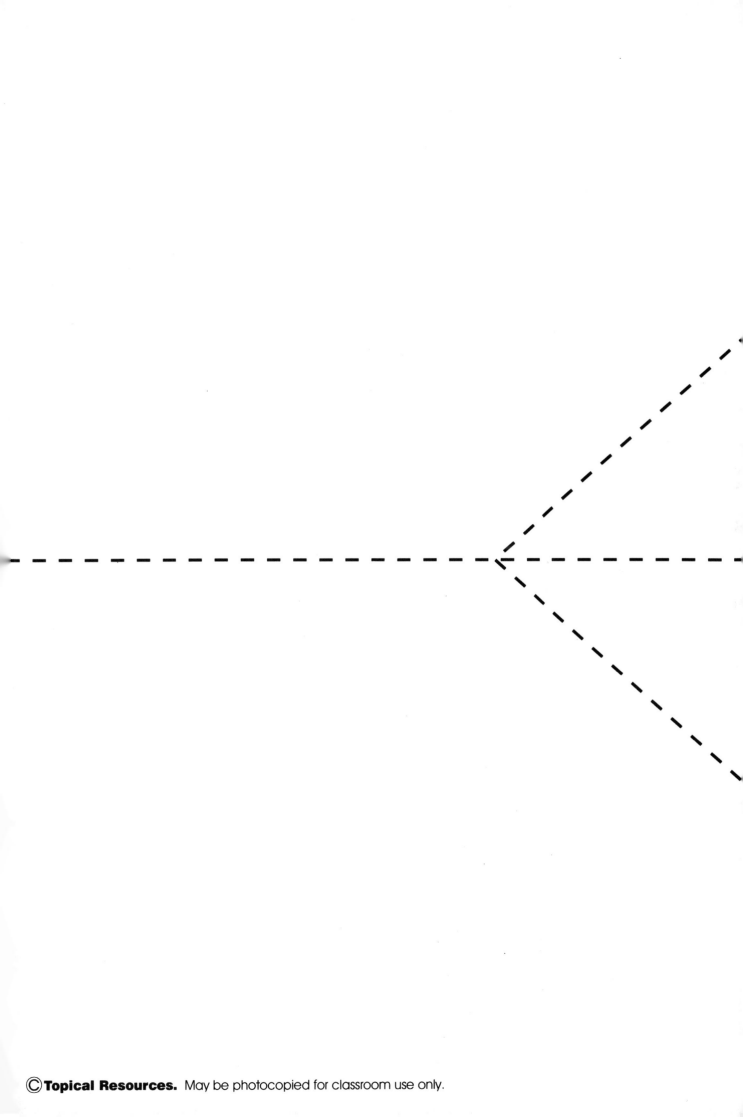

Rocking Horse Card

Technique used:
    Rocking card

Equipment needed:
    scissors
    card
    glue sticks
    teacher prepared circles

How to make the example:

Step 1. Photocopy the sheet opposite onto card or use templates to create the shapes, one per child.
Step 2. Draw around the template onto card and cut out the rocking horse.
Step 3. Cut out the circle and fold in half down the central dotted line.
Step 4. Decorate the rocking horse picture and stick it to the outside of the rocking card along the top fold.
Step 5. The pupils will now have a card that rocks.
Step 6. Write the card message on the rocking base.

How the idea may be developed.

The basic rocking card design can be used for different occassions e.g. Christmas trees, Christmas candles etc. An alternative design could incorporate parallel cuts - see later in the book. This would create a rocking semi-circular card which when opened pops - up into a simple scene e.g.

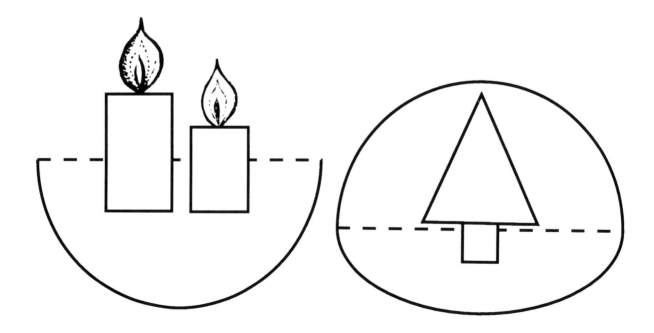

Extending Snake Card

Technique used:

Spiral cut

Equipment needed:
scissors
glue sticks
felt pens or coloured crayons
card

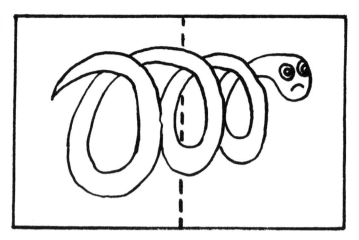

How to make the example

Step 1. Photocopy the shape below onto card or paste onto card, one per child.
Step 2. Fold an A4 sheet of card in half as shown on the opposite page.
Step 3. Colour in the snake shape and cut it out.
Step 4. Cut along the spiralling decreasing line drawn through the snake.
Step 5. Stick the head to A on the inside of the card.
Step 6. Stick the tail to B on the opposite side of the card.
Step 7. Decorate the front of the card by creating patterns and using colours similar
to those used to decorate the snake

How the idea may be developed.

For the best effect the pupils can decorate both sides of the un-cut snake.
Once the technique has been introduced then the pupils should be encouraged to
create their own pop-up cards using snakes or other creatures of their own design.

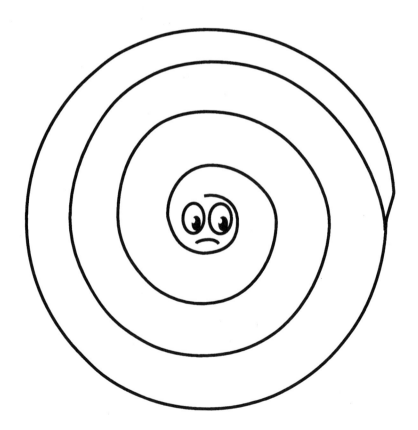

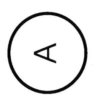

Mother's Day Card

Technique used:
> One cut pop - up.

Equipment Needed:
> scissors
> glue sticks
> assorted papers cut into flower shapes
> card
> papers
> teacher made example

How to make the example:

Step 1.   Photocopy the sheet opposite onto card or stick onto card, one per child.
Step 2.   Fold the card in half.
Step 3.   Cut along the unbroken line from A to B
Step 4.   Fold from the end of the cut line [B] to the centre fold along the dotted line. Fold about 10 times in and out finally leaving the triangle shape inside the card.
Step 5.   Show the pupils a finished card and let them decorate their card in a similar way yet with free choice of the papers from which their flowers are made. Please note! The flowers are attached to the background of the card, not the pop - up.
Step 6.   Back the cut by sticking a rectangular piece of paper over the folded spine Make sure the paper is slightly bigger than the cut and the fold.
Step 7.   Cover the outside of the card using paper chosen by the pupil and decorate using the same colours and similar theme to the inside.

Remember:
You will have a class of cards which will demonstrate that all the pupils have experienced the same technique yet each pupil will have contributed in an individual way and they will know / recognise their own card.

How the idea may be developed:
Limit their colour choice. Suggest:-   2 colours + black + white; colour families; warm colours; cold colours etc.....
Encourage the pupils to create a front cover design using similar colours and the same theme, on a separate piece of paper to be mounted on the backing paper.

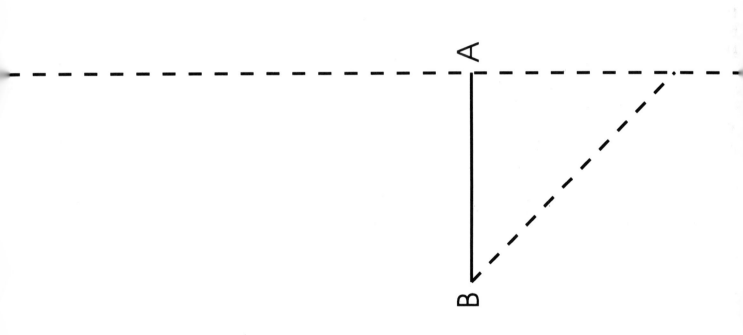

A

B

Christmas Tree Card

Technique Used:
> One cut pop - up.

Equipment needed:
> scissors
> card
> glue sticks
> collage materials
> teacher made example

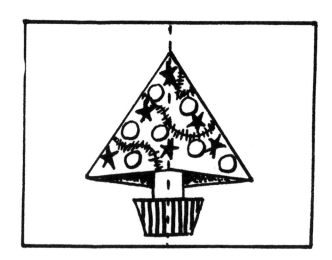

How to make the example:

Step 1.   Photocopy the sheet opposite onto card or stick onto card, one per child.

Step 2.   Fold the card in half and cut along the unbroken line from A to B.

Step 3.   Fold from the end of the cut [B] to the centre fold line down the dotted line. Fold about ten times in and out finally leaving the triangle shape inside the card.

Step 4.   Cover the pop - up tree shape with a patterned piece of paper. First, let the pupils choose the paper from a selection prepared by the teacher and fold down the centre. The cut card can be used as a template. Place the template over the folded patterned paper making sure the folded spines are in line. Cut out the triangular shape and stick in place on the pop-up tree.

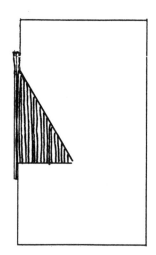

Step 5.   Apply additional finishing techniques.

Step 6.   Back and decorate the front of the card.

How the idea may be developed.

This cut can be of varying sizes and in a variety of positions along the folded spine to create a variety of cards for different occasions using this technique.

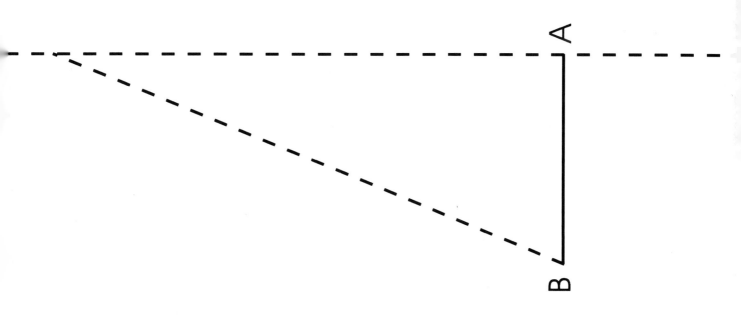

A

B

Christmas Cracker Card

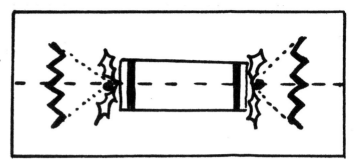

Technique used:
>   One cut pop - up technique, twice.

Equipment Needed:
>   scissors
>   glue sticks
>   felt pens and crayons
>   card
>   papers
>   teacher prepared example

How to make the example:

Step 1.   Photocopy the sheet opposite onto card or stick onto card.
Step 2.   Fold the card in half along the dotted line.
Step 3.   Cut with scissors along the zig zag lines marked with the wider solid lines.
Step 4.   Fold along the dotted lines forwards and backwards 10 times, leaving the shapes inside the card.
Step 5.   Let the pupils colour in the card using felt pens, crayons etc...
Step 6.   Back the card and decorate the front cover using colours and themes similar to the ones inside.

How the idea may be developed:

The pupils could print a greeting for the inside / outside of the card using a word processor. The pupils can all be introduced to the same skill yet choose from a variety of designs which the teacher has drawn. Parallel cuts can be used to make the centre of the cracker pop-up as well

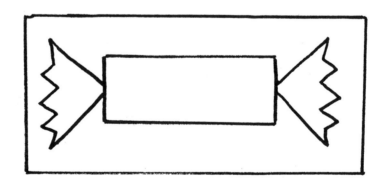

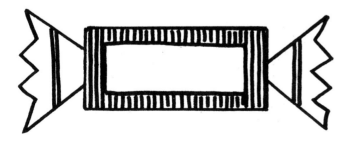

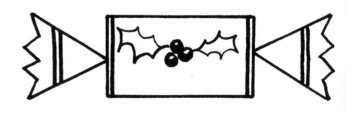

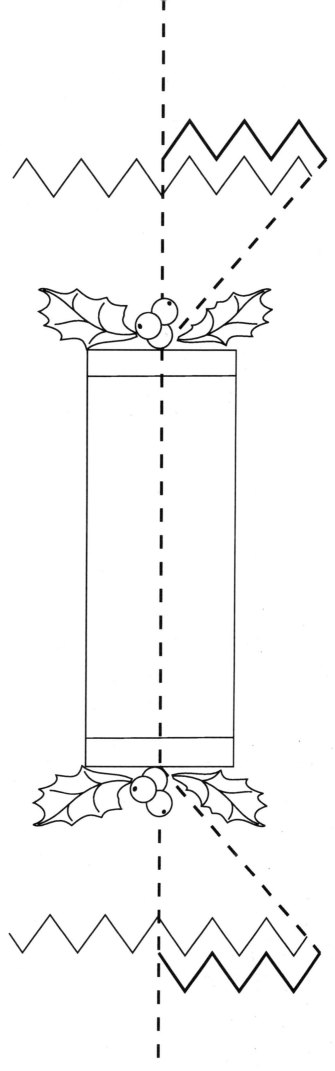

Talking Animal Card

Technique used:
> One cut pop - up with 2 folds.

Equipment needed:
> scissors
> card
> felt pens and crayons
> manufactured pop - up books
> teacher made example
> selection of papers
> glue sticks

How to make the example:

Step 1. Photocopy the sheet opposite onto card or stick onto card, one per child.

Step 2. Fold the card in half and cut along the straight line in the centre of the mouth.

Step 3. Fold along the dotted lines from the end of the cut to the folded spine of the card about 10 times forwards and backwards leaving the triangle shapes inside the card.

Step 4. Let the pupils decide on the colours and finishing techniques to decorate the animal.

Step 5. Back the cut with a rectangular piece of paper, slightly larger than the cut which the teacher has prepared.

Step 6. Let the pupils select paper to back the card and design a front cover.

How the idea may be developed:

The cut can be of any length and the folds can vary in size according to the size of the mouth on the creature being created.

A class book can be created with groups of children designing and making one animal.

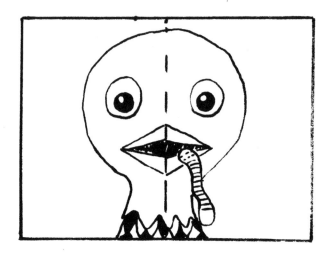

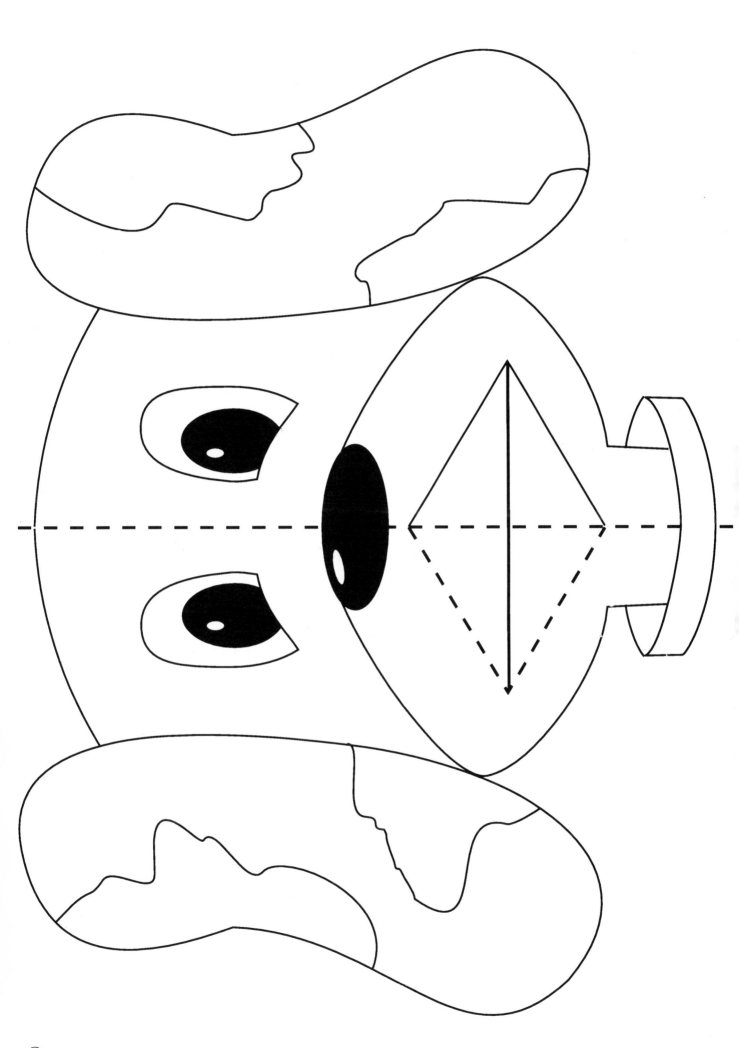

Mini - Beasts Card

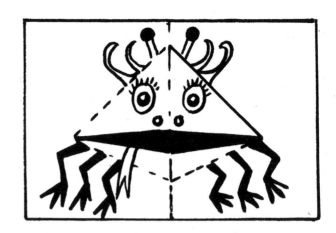

Technique used:
One cut pop - up with 2 folds.

Equipment needed:
scissors
card
collage materials
manufactured pop - up books
design sheet
felt pens and crayons
glue sticks

How to make the example:
Step 1. Photocopy the sheet opposite onto card or stick onto card, one per child.
Step 2. Let the pupils fold the card in half and cut along the straight unbroken line across the mouth.
Step 3. Help the pupils fold along the dotted lines drawn from the end of the cut to the folded spine of the card. Fold forwards and backwards about 10 times leaving the triangle shapes inside the card.
Step 4. Decorate the mini - beast.
Step 5. Back the cut and the card and decorate the front cover.

How the idea may be developed:

Before the pupils decorate a card using this technique, they could design their mini - beast on a design sheet. They can gain inspiration from the manufactured pop - up books on mini - beasts, actual mini - beasts or pictures. The design can then be transferred onto a mini - beast card.
The pupils can cut their own mouth shapes, maybe instead of a straight line they could cut a zig zag line to create teeth.
Printing shapes on the mini - beasts can create interesting patterns.

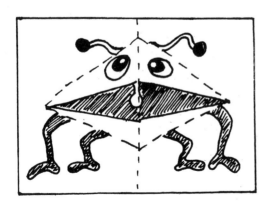

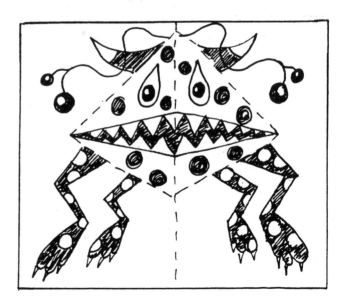

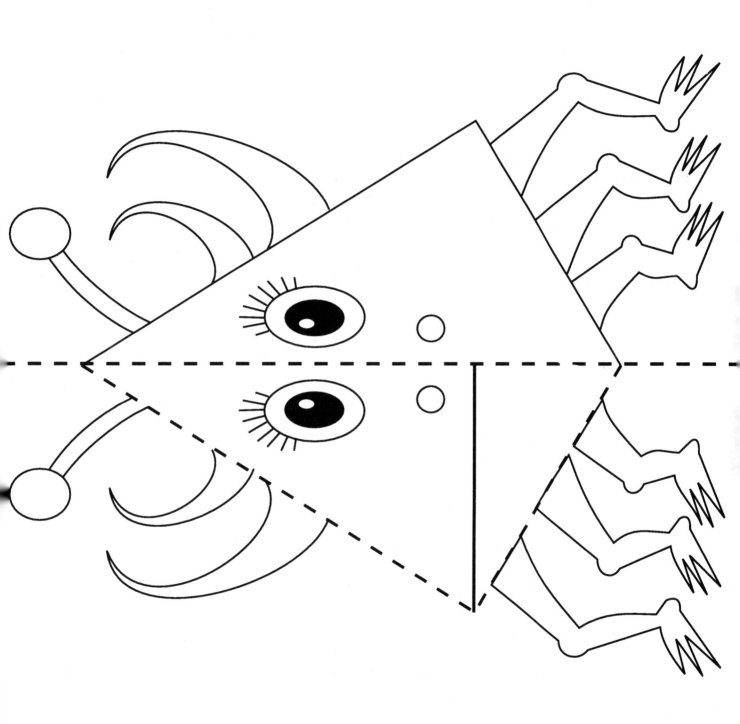

Frog Card

Technique used:
>One cut pop - up with 2 folds.

Equipment needed:
>scissors
>card
>collage materials
>felt pens and crayons
>glue sticks

How to make the example:

Step 1. Photocopy the sheet opposite onto card or stick onto card, one per child.
Step 2. Fold the card in half and cut out the frog shape.
Step 3. Cut along the unbroken line drawn across the centre of the frogs mouth.
Step 4. Fold along the dotted lines from the end of the cut to the folded centre line of the frog. Fold about 10 times in and out until the mouth easily pops open.
Step 5. Decorate the frog.
Step 6. Back the mouth cut in red paper and stick the completed frog into the centre of a folded sheet of A4 card, the pupils should choose the colour.
Step 7. Decorate the front of the card in similar colours and a theme connected with the pop - up.

How the idea may be developed:

For a card featuring an animal the pupils need to be taught how to cut shapes out so that they are symmetrical as they are far more effective and the finished card is of a higher quality.

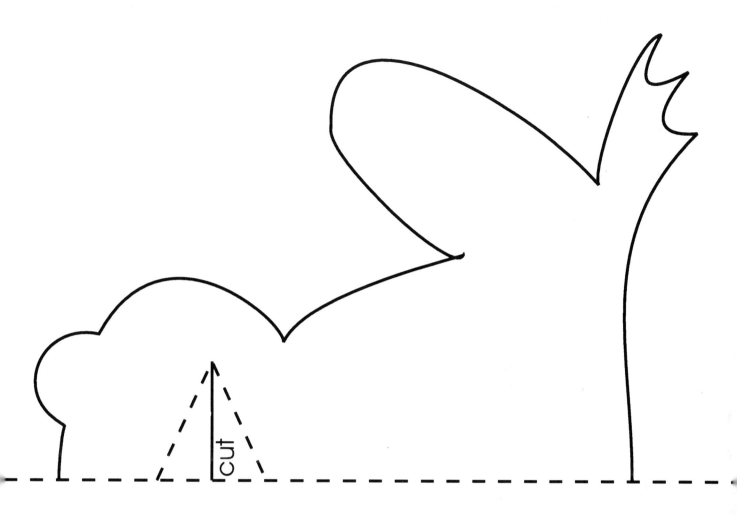

cut

Face Card

Technique used:
> One cut pop - up with one fold
> and one cut pop - up with 2 folds.

Equipment needed:
> scissors
> card
> glue stick
> felt pens
> collage materials
> selection of papers

How to make the example:

Step 1. Photocopy the sheet opposite onto card.

Step 2. Fold the card in half and cut out the face shape.

Step 3. Keep the face shape folded and cut along the two unbroken lines, one to form the nose and the other to form the mouth pop - up.

Step 4. Fold along the dotted lines which are drawn from the ends of the cuts to the folded centre line of the face about 10 times finally leaving the triangle shapes inside the card.

Step 5. Let the pupils decorate the face using felt pens and collage materials.

Step 6. Once the decorated face is dry then the mouth and nose cut should be backed using suitably coloured paper and the face can be stuck in the centre of a piece of A4 card. Let the pupils select the colour.

Step 7. Decorate the outside of the card and create a message for the inside.

How the idea may be developed:

The face shape can be cut out of coloured card, the children need to be taught how to cut out symmetrical shapes.

This is an ideal way to combine card engineering with descriptive writing in English as the faces can be made to fit a description in a book e.g. The Twits.

The faces can be described by the pupils that created them after completion and an identikit game can be created by trying to match the face to the correct piece of writing.

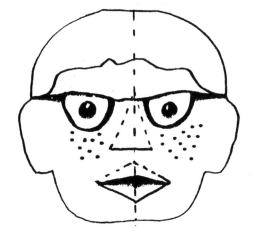
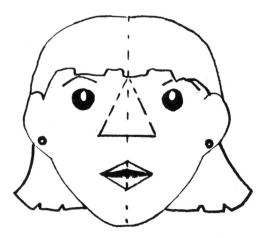

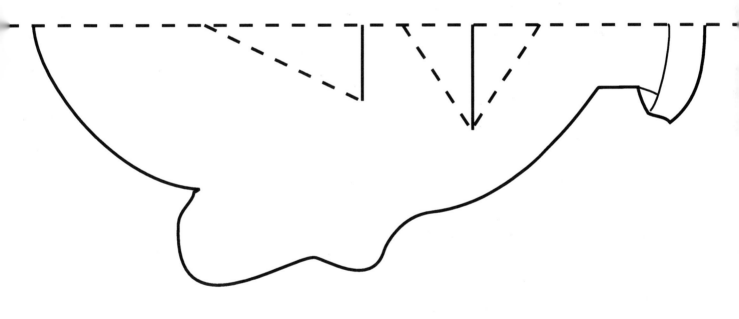

Closing Eyes Card

Technique used:

One cut pop - up with 2 folds - twice

Equipment needed:

scissors
card
felt pens and crayons
glue sticks
assorted papers

How to make the example:

Step 1. Photocopy the sheet opposite onto card or stick onto card, one per child.

Step 2. Fold the card in half along the dotted line which runs from top to bottom and cut out the animals head.

Step 3. Unfold the animals head and refold the card across the centre of the eyes, where the dotted line is drawn.

Step 4. Cut along the 2 solid lines drawn in the position of the eyes and fold from the ends of the cuts along the four dotted lines.

Step 5. Press the fold in well by folding backwards and forwards and running your finger along the crease line finally leaving the triangle shapes inside the card.

Step 6. Back the eye cuts with white paper and either draw or stick in the centres of the eyes.

Step 7. Decorate the head and then glue it into the centre of a piece of A4 paper or card which has been selected by the pupil.

Step 8. Decorate the outside of the card remembering that this card opens from the top to the bottom with the folded edge across the top.

How the idea may be developed:

The freedom in the decoration must be provided for by the range of materials provided. Once the cut has been introduced then the children must experiment on cheap paper or used cards to perfect their design for an animals head and the eye positions.

This can be introduced to a class by giving them the photocopiable sheets. They can then develop the idea for a Christmas Card and create a variety of characters and animals with opening eyes: e.g. Reindeer, robins, snowmen, penguins, Father Christmas, Angels etc..

24

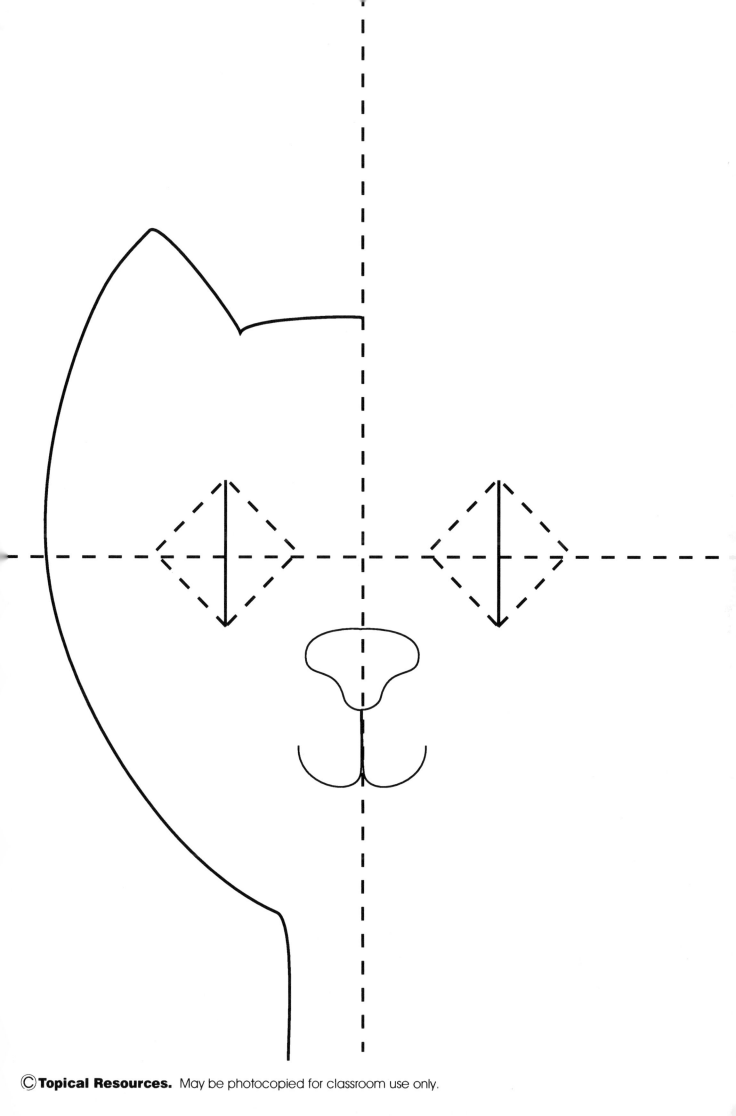

Valentine Card

Technique used:
>   Curved line cut and fold.

Eqipment needed.
>   scissors
>   glue
>   assorted reclaimed papers
>   card

How to make the example:

Step 1. Photocopy the sheet opposite onto card or stick onto card, one per child.

Step 2. Fold the card in half and cut along the unbroken curved line.

Step 3. Fold from the end of the cut curved line to the centre fold of the card about 10 times finally leaving the heart shape on the inside of the card.

Step 4. Decorate the card using teacher prepared heart shapes cut from an assortment of reclaimed papers. A selection of sizes should be available for the pupils to select from.

Step 5. Back the cut heart shape and cover the outside of the card.

Step 6. Discuss and decorate the front cover of the card.

How the idea may be developed.

Variations of the above card can be created by creating three heart shapes down the centre fold increasing in size from the top of the card.

Older pupils can be encouraged to cut the heart shapes themselves for decoration or you may wish the pupils to colour a design on the pop - up hearts.

Because of the simplicity of the shape created, great variations can be achieved when decorating the front cover.

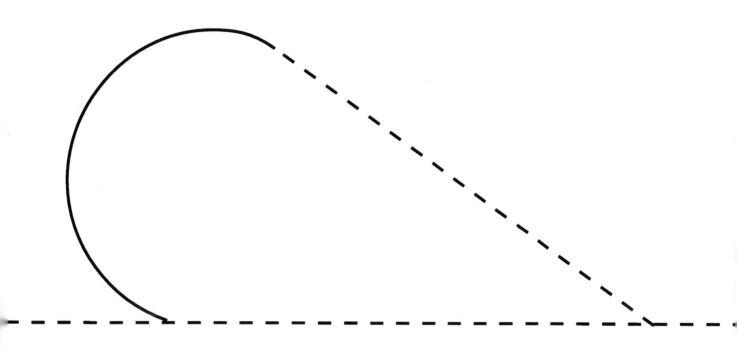

Pop-Up Nose Card

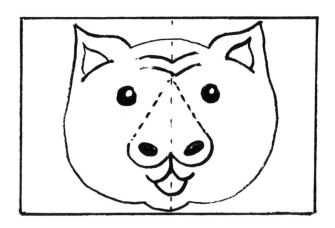

Technique used:

    Curved line cut with one fold.

Equipment needed:

    scissors
    card
    felt pens and crayons
    glue sticks
    collage materials
    papers of varying sizes and colours

How to make the example:

Step 1. Photocopy the sheet opposite onto card or stick onto card, one per child.

Step 2. Fold the card in half and cut out the animal's head. Next cut along the unbroken line drawn under the nose shape to form the pop-up nose.

Step 3. Fold down the dotted lines drawn from the end of the cut to the centre fold of the card about 10 times finally leaving the inverted heart shape on the inside of the card.

Step 4. Decorate the card to create the pig with a pop - up nose.

Step 5. Stick the backing paper over the nose cut and glue head inside an A4 folded card shape..

Step 6. Discuss with the pupils the type of decoration which is to be placed on the front cover and then finish the card.

How the idea may be developed.

This cut can be used to create group or class books on a variety of topics:- My Family, My Friends, Old Mac Donald etc. When the larger pages e.g. A3 size, have been created and backed, they should be stuck together with either glue or tape around the edges. Remember to bind the spine of the book with strong tape - carpet tape works very well and can be obtained in a variety of colours.

Make sure that the pages are large enough to ensure a successful class / group book and that 2 - 4 pupils can work on each page.

Combine word processing skills so that the finished book is of a high standard.

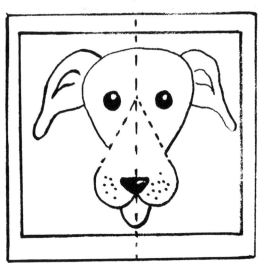

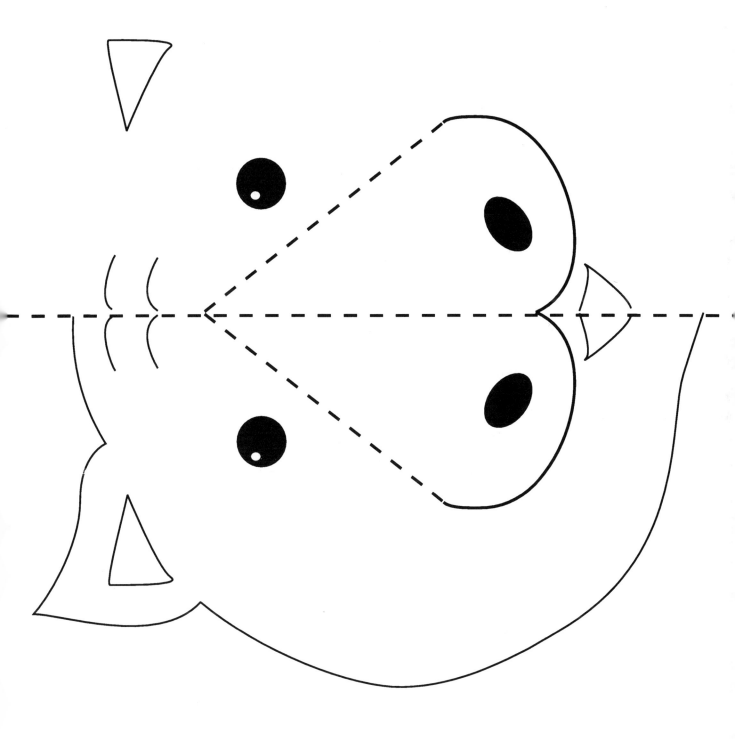

Standing Christmas Card

Technique used:
 Parallel Cuts.

Equipment needed:
 scissors
 card
 felt pens and crayons
 an assortment of reclaimed or
 plain and decorated papers
 glue sticks
 stars
 sequins

How to make the example:

Step 1. Photocopy the sheet opposite onto card or stick onto card, one per child.
Step 2. Fold the large sheet of card in half along the dotted line.
Step 3. Cut along the 2 solid parallel lines drawn near the centre of the card which are
 of equal length.
Step 4. Fold along the dotted line drawn from the ends of the cuts. Fold backwards and
 forwards along this line about ten times to ensure the success of the pop - up
 finally leaving the pop - up tabs on the inside of the card.
Step 5. Decorate the inside of the card. The sky needs to be painted or coloured and so
 does the ground. When the background is dry let the pupils stick into the night
 sky stars or sequins.
Step 6. Use the triangle shape at the bottom of this sheet as a template and provide a
 selection of papers which the pupils can choose from to draw around the
 template onto to create their pop - up tree.
Step 7. Stick the previously prepared tree onto the pop - up tab near the bottom of the
 tab ensuring that it does not stick out over the edge of the folded card.
Step 8. Back the card and decorate the front cover.
 Remember! - This card opens in a different way than the others, the front cover
 of the card must be decorated accordingly.

How the idea may be developed.

This is perhaps the most versatile of the
simple cuts which can and should be
introduced to Key Stage 1 pupils or to
pupils with little or no experience of
making pop-up cards.
A variety of scenes can be created
from the parallel cuts which can
vary in length and width according
to the design and purpose.
e.g. a standing snowman, robin
or Easter rabbit.

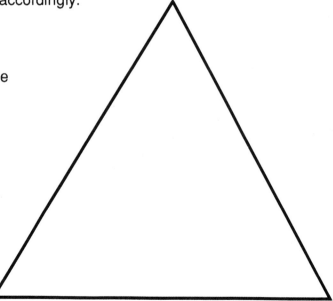

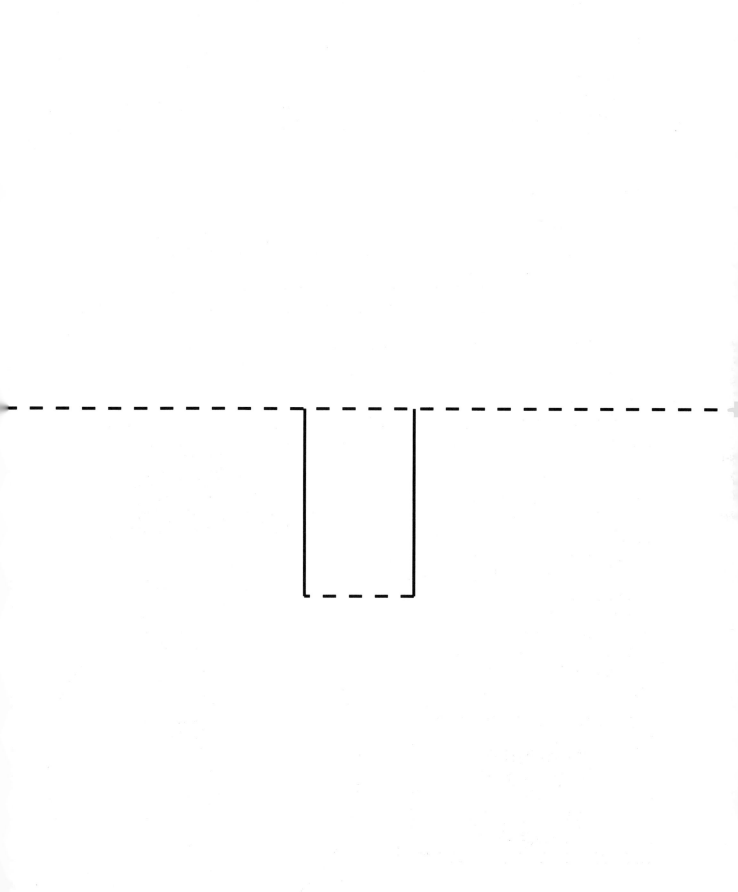

Pop-Up Snowman Card

Technique used:
Parallel cuts

Equipment needed:
scissors
glue sticks
card
collage materials
felt pens
paints

How to make the example:

Step 1. Photocopy the sheet opposite onto card or stick onto card, one per child.
Step 2. Fold the card in half and cut along the 2 parallel unbroken lines drawn near the centre of the card.
Step 3. Fold along the dotted line drawn between the two parallel cuts.
Step 4. The pupils should decorate the background of the card. This can be painted, coloured or printed.
Step 5. Photocopy the snowman shape at the bottom of this page and use as a template for the pupils or the teachers to draw around and cut out a snowman, one per child.
Step 6. Decorate the snowman and when dry fold in half and stick onto the pop - up section of the background as in the diagram above.
Step 7. Back the card and decorate the front cover continuing with the same theme and colours.

How the idea may be developed.

Supply a variety of collected old Christmas cards - the need for forward planning is essential. From this collection the pupils can select an image to cut out and stick to the centre pop - up.
Another way to use this technique to its best advantage is to combine work produced with a word processor to create a pop - up Christmas message.

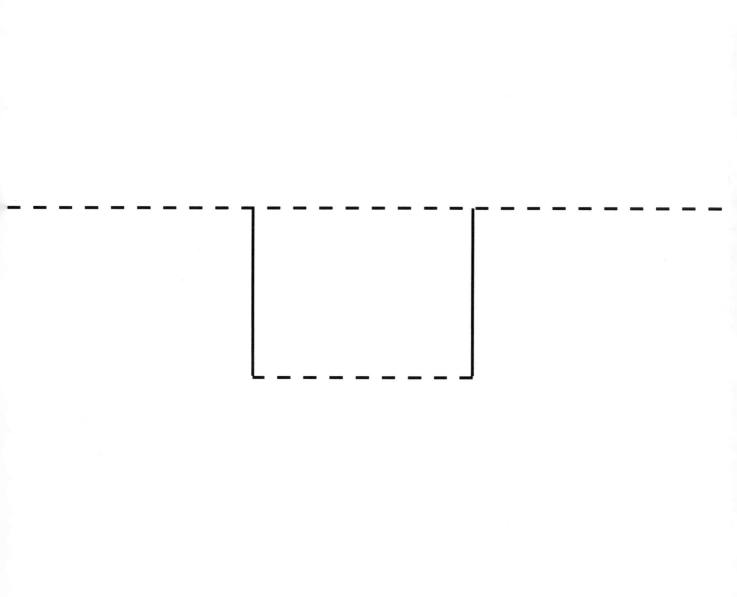

Card Engineering skills for KEY STAGE 2

Parallel Cuts at 45⁰

This cut can be introduced within mathematics work as it requires the use of standard measurements - centimetres and degrees. The pupils need to have had previous experience with cutting and folding to achieve quality results.

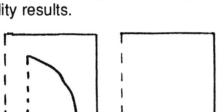

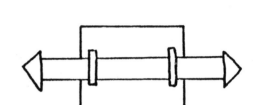

Cut Out and Hinged Windows

These techniques can be used to introduce individual pupils to the use of a craft knife, safety ruler and cutting mat. The technique is also effective when using a folded piece of A3 paper to create an A5 sized card.

Sliding Rods

The first step to introducing pupils to straight line motion. Pupils need to be introduced to guiding loops and this technique involves them creating two loops to guide the rod.

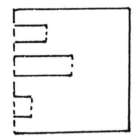

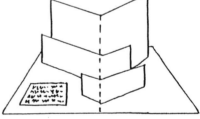

Multiple Parallel Cuts

A development to the simple parallel cuts introduced in Key Stage 1. Once the children have been taught the technique then they can create a variety of scenes with depth.

Dioramas

A wonderful and exciting technique to create cards that stand at a 90⁰ angle to the base. Once the pupils have been taught how to create a diorama then the technique can be incorporated into a variety of topic work to represent factual and fictional scenes.

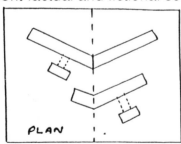

PLAN

Pull-Ups

This technique is dependant upon the pupils being able to create a diorama and they need to be able to measure with some degree of accuracy to ensure success. The Pull-ups will only work if attached to the diorama pieces.

Levers

Pupils should be given the opportunity to experiment with a variety of levers. Can they discover everyday objects that use levers in order to function? Examples could be scissors, see-saws etc..

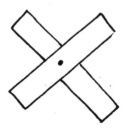

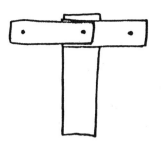

T - Shaped Levers

A versatile technique to enable equal movement using levers connected opposite each other on a central strip.

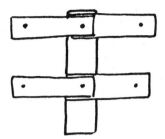

Multiple T-Shaped Levers

A versatile way of gaining movement in cards and books, the principles of which can then be transferred to other stiff sheet materials. The close links with science should be emphasised.

Linkages

When a series of levers are connected they become linkages. Many different forms of movement can be created using a variety of strips joined and guided with guiding loops.

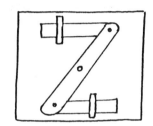

Z Shaped Linkages

This will demonstrate to pupils how a fixed pivot can create movement in a straight line yet on different levels when using levers.

Parallel Linkages

One way of creating movement of equal size yet in opposite directions.

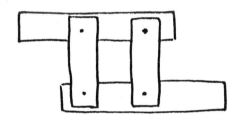

Straight Line Slots

Pupils should cut the slots and this will involve the use of a craft knife, safety ruler and cutting mat, all of which should previously have been introduced in a safe and structured manner due to the safety aspects. The slots can be horizontal, vertical or diagonal depending on the individual pupil's design.

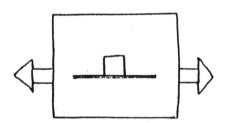

Circular Motion

Many manufactured pop - up books will feature circular motion and this can be introduced in a simple yet effective way by using levers and fixed pivots.

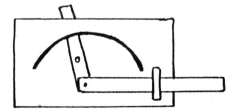

Reverse Fold Card

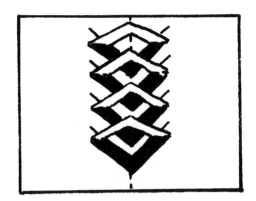

Technique Used:
  Parallel Cuts at 45

Equipment needed:
  scissors
  assorted papers A4 size
  glue sticks

How To Make The Example:

Step 1. Photocopy the sheet opposite, one per child.
Step 2. Fold down the middle dotted line and cut along the solid lines with a pair of scissors.
Step 3. Open the card and fold the alternate cuts upwards.
          If a piece of coloured A4 paper is folded and placed inside the photocopied sheet prior to folding, then when the cuts are folded upwards, the different colour on the reverse side will be revealed.
Step 4. Back the card in a contrasting colour and decorate the front cover.

How the idea may be developed.

This cut should then be experimented with:
• use two sheets of paper in different colours
• card or paper which is a different colour on the reverse side
• combine the cuts in different directions

An effective use is to form a Christmas Tree:

This cut can create bookmarks, place mats, coasters (cover with sticky backed plastic), Christmas cards and calendars.

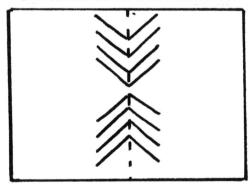

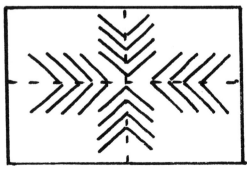

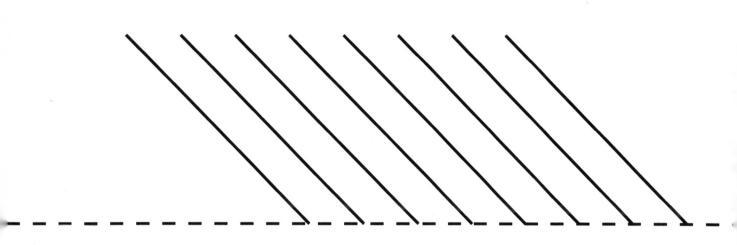

Cut Out Window Cards

Technique used:

Cut out and hinged windows

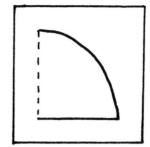

Equipment needed:

scissors
craft knife
cutting mat
safety ruler
glue
felt pens, crayons
assortment of papers A4 in size

How to make the Example:

Step 1. Photocopy the sheet opposite onto coloured card or stiff paper, one per child.
Step 2. Cut down the centre unbroken line to create 2 card fronts.
Step 3. Using the Star Card :   Show the pupils how to push the end of a pair of scissors through the centre of the shape you require cutting out. Let them cut around the line to create a star shaped window.
Step 4. Using the Hinged Card: Demonstrate to the pupils how to use a craft knife and a cutting mat. Cut along the 2 unbroken lines and fold along the dotted line to create a card front with a hinged window.
Step 5. On a folded piece of card [A4 in size] the pupils can draw through the created windows to find the required position for their design.
Step 6. Once the design is completed then the decorated window front should be glued in position on the front of the card and a message written on the inside. Ideas for decorating the window front could include marbling, printing or covering with Christmas wrapping paper etc.

How the idea may be developed:

The pupils can be given the freedom to create their own front window designs. Shapes chosen could be used to reflect the type of greetings card that the pupils are making e.g   An Egg shape for an Easter card; a Christmas Tree shape for a Christmas card; a heart shape for a Valentine's card etc....

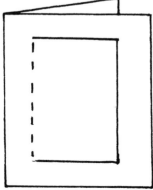
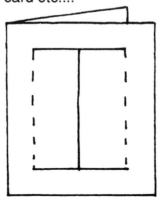
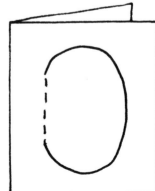

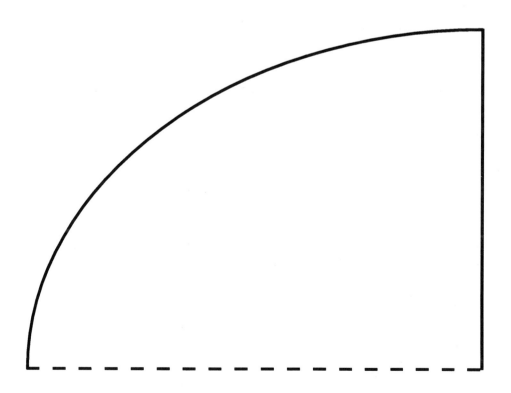

Many Eyed Snowman Card

Technique Used:
Sliding Rods

Equipment needed:
scissors
felt pens and crayons
craft knife
cutting mat
glue stick

How to make the example:

Step 1.   Photocopy the sheet opposite onto card or stick onto card, one per child.
Step 2.   Cut out the snowman and decorate.
Step 3.   The teacher must cut out the eye holes with a craft knife and cutting mat or show the pupils how to cut out a centre shape by pushing the ends of a pointed pair of scissors through the centre and carefully cutting around the edge.
Step 4.   Cut out the strip B and paste onto thick card.
Step 5.   Make the control loops by cutting out, folding along the dotted lines and gluing the third section into position on top of the first folded section forming a loop. Position the loops over the sliding rod. Position the eyes and glue the loops in place on the reverse side of the snowman's head so that they will guide the rod. Glue triangular end stops onto the rod. Pushing and pulling the rod will make the snowman's eyes move.
Step 6.   The snowman can then be glued to a piece of decorated backing card and a suitable message added to form a greetings card.

How the idea may be developed:

This technique is useful for greetings cards and also for teaching aids. When creating visual aids for teaching remember to make the card larger so that the pupils can see the pictures or symbols in the windows.

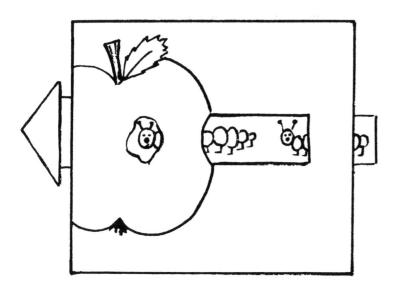

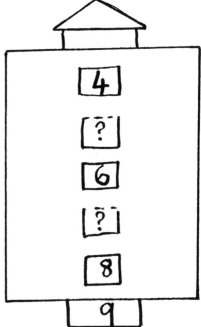

control loops

3D Easter Card

Technique used:

Multiple Parallel Cuts

Equipment needed

scissors
glue
felt pens, crayons

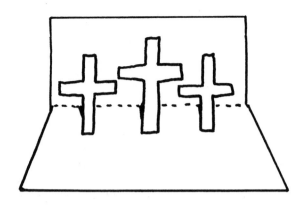

How to make the example:

Step 1. Photocopy the sheet opposite onto card, one per child; or use as a template
Step 2. Fold the sheet in half along the dotted line.
Step 3. Using scissors the pupils should cut along the parallel solid lines - 6 cuts.
Step 4. Once these lines have been cut then the pupils must fold along the dotted lines pressing the folds in well.
Step 5. The 3 stepped cuts will now pop - up if the card is reversed and the pupils should at this stage decorate the background.
Step 6. Photocopy the crosses on this sheet and use as templates.
Step 7. The pupils can cdraw around the templates onto plain paper which will need decorating or onto patterned paper of their choice.
Step 8. The decorated crosses are then glued onto the stepped pop - ups as in the above diagram.

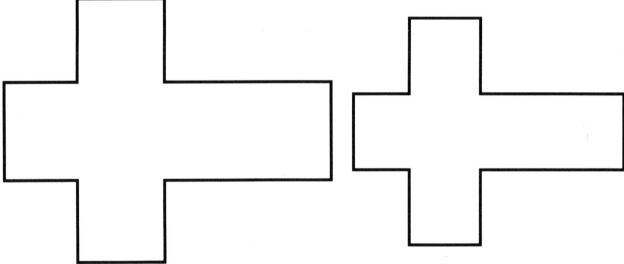

How the idea may be developed:

Instead of three parallel cuts, the pupils can make as many as required in a variety of lengths. Topic work can be illustrated in this way; pictures drawn by the pupils can be mounted onto the pop - ups to produce a scene which has depth and writing can be mounted on the base to produce for example an Egyptian scene.

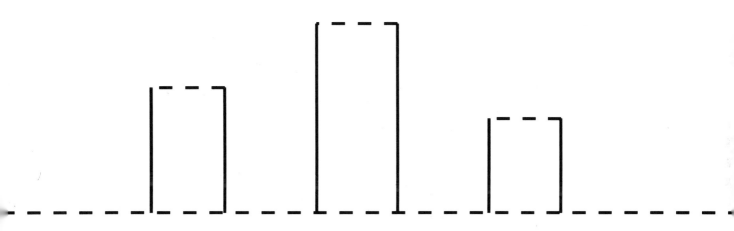

3D Castle Card

Technique Used:
>A Diorama

Equipment needed:
>scissors
>felt pens and crayons
>glue sticks
>manufactured books and cards containing dioramas
>teacher made examples

How to make the example:

Step 1. Photocopy the sheet opposite onto card or stick onto card, one per child.
Step 2. Cut along the centre solid line and fold A in half along the dotted line, decorate to create the ground of the scene.
Step 3. Cut out the castle shape and decorate. Fold in half along the dotted line.
Step 4. Cut out the shaded triangle area.
Step 5. Fold the tabs inwards along the dotted line.
Step 6. Glue down the bottom flaps of the castle onto the marked areas on A.
>(Glue sticks - the Pritt type - are the best but pupils should experiment to see which type of glue is the most appropriate).
>The insert will now stand vertically.
Step 7. Cut out the dragon and fold down the centre line. Cut off the shaded triangle area.
Step 8. Fold the tab inward along the dotted line.
Step 9. Glue down the bottom flaps of the dragon onto the marked areas on A. When A is folded along the dotted line then the shapes will lie down flat.
Step 10. Back the card and decorate the front cover.

How the idea may be developed.

The pupils can create dioramas to represent any scene required.
It is up to the pupil to decide how many levels will be created in the card when they design their own. The levels of the scene should increase in size from the front to the rear of the scene.
The inserts do not have to be equal in size on each side of the fold but they do have to have a fold in them.

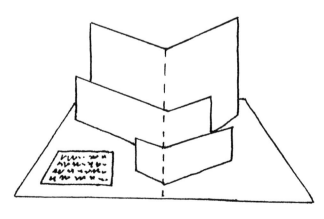

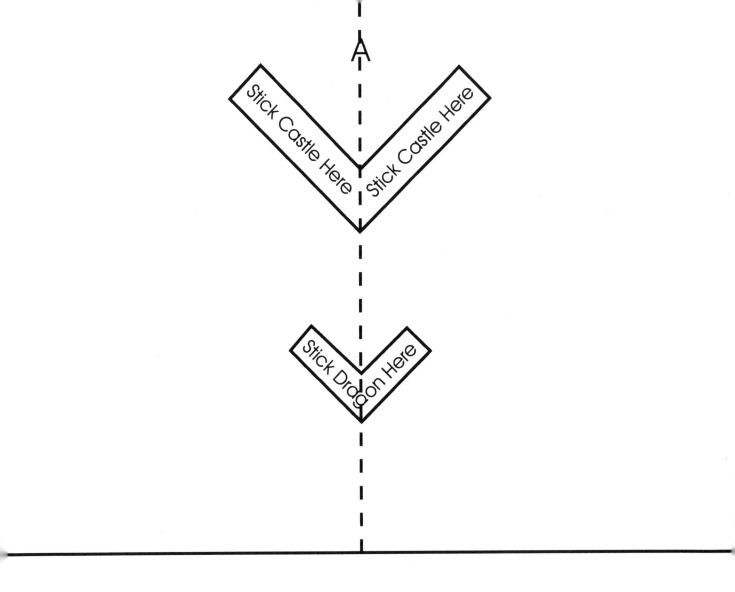

A

Stick Castle Here   Stick Castle Here

Stick Dragon Here

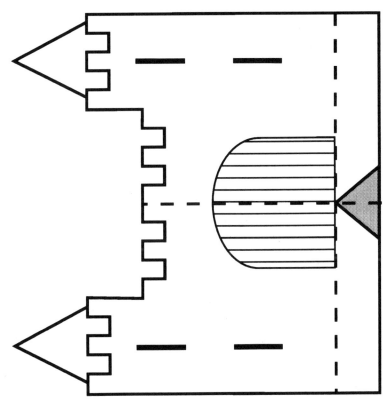

3D Forest Card

Technique Used:
   Pull Ups

Equipment needed:
   scissors
   card
   glue stick
   felt pens and crayons

How to make the example:

Step 1. Photocopy the sheet opposite, one per child.

Step 2. Cut the sheet in half along the solid black line and then fold A in half.

Step 3. Cut out the shapes along the solid black lines and decorate them. The rectangular strip should be folded along the dotted lines.

Step 4. Fold the hedge in half and cut off the shaded triangle.

Step 5. Fold the tabs inwards and stick to the marked area on A

Step 6. Fold along the dotted line between the rabbit and the tab and stick onto A where marked.

Step 7. Glue the strip to the back of the rabbit and the front of the hedge where indicated with the dotted rectangular shapes. This will enable the hedge to pull up the rabbit shape when the card is opened.

Step 8. Decorate the base of the card and when it is closed the shapes will lie down flat.

Step 9. Design a front cover for the card.

How the idea may be developed.

Additional dioramas can be added to pupils own designs for scenes and pull-ups attached to each one. N.B The pull-ups must run parallel to the dioramas.

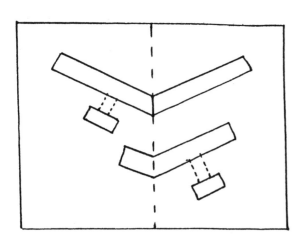

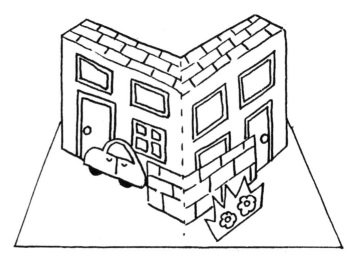

Stick the Hedge Here

A

Rabbit

Strip

Extending Hand Card

Technique Used:

Levers

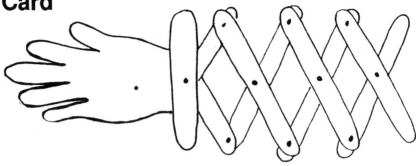

A **lever** is a bar / rod that swings / pivots around a fixed point. When one part of the bar is moved the other side moves also - only the fixed point stays in the same place.

Linkages: 2 or more levers joined together.

Equipment needed:

scissors
thick card
11 brass fasteners
hole punch / paper drill

How to make the example:

Step 1.   Photocopy the sheet opposite, one per child and glue onto card.
Step 2.   Cut out the 8 strips A - H and make small holes with the pointed end of a pair of scissors over the dots on the strips. Fasten together using brass fasteners as in the diagram.
Step 3.   Cut out the hand and fasten to G with brass fasteners through the holes marked i and ii on the hand and on the strip. Match up the corresponding holes on the hand and on the strip, i to i, ii to ii. Operate the hand.

How the idea may be developed:

The pupils should create their own end addition and attach it to the linkages.
A greeting could be written on the extending hand or the pop - up linkage could be placed inside a pocket of a conventional card.

The pupils can experiment with different
lengths of linkages. e.g.
    How will 6 or 4 strips fastened
    together operate?
    How will 10 or 12 strips
    fastened together operate?

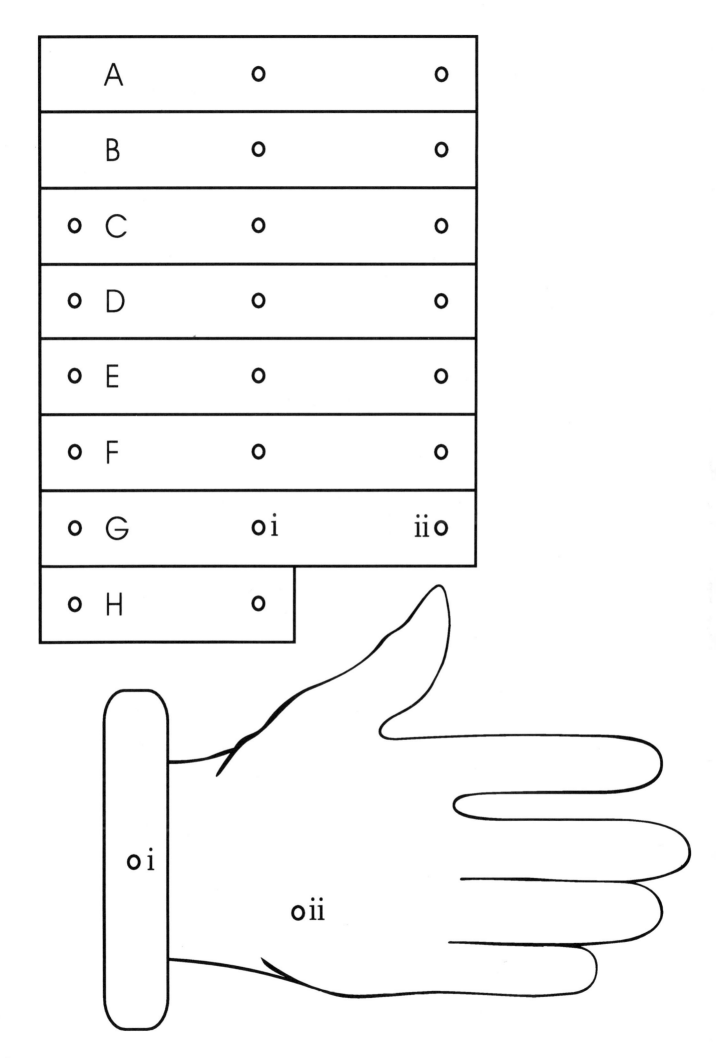

Moving Scarecrow Card

Technique Used:

T Shaped Levers

Equipment needed:

scissors
card
felt pens or coloured crayons
3 brass fasteners
hole punch or paper drill

How to make the example:

Step 1. Photocopy the sheet opposite onto card or paste onto card, one per child.
Step 2. Cut out the 2 arms and colour in and cut out strip A.
Step 3. Cut out the scarecrow.
Step 4. Colour in the scarecrow.
Step 5. Fasten the arms and A together at the holes marked i.
Step 6. Position A at right angles to the arms and fasten the arms on the reverse side of the scarecrow picture through the centre of the X's.
Step 7. Make the guiding loop by cutting it out and folding it along the dotted lines. Stick the card to create a loop.
Step 8. Position the guiding loop over the rod A and stick the loop to the reverse side of the card.
Step 9. By pulling A down and pushing it up, the scarecrows arms will move.
Step 9. Glue the scarecrow by the head to the front of an A4 folded card and add a suitable greeting.

How the idea may be developed:

Let the pupils use the techniques they have practiced to create their own moving picture, hanging toy or Christmas tree decoration.
Children can investigate if more movement be gained in the arms by changing the position of the brass fasteners.

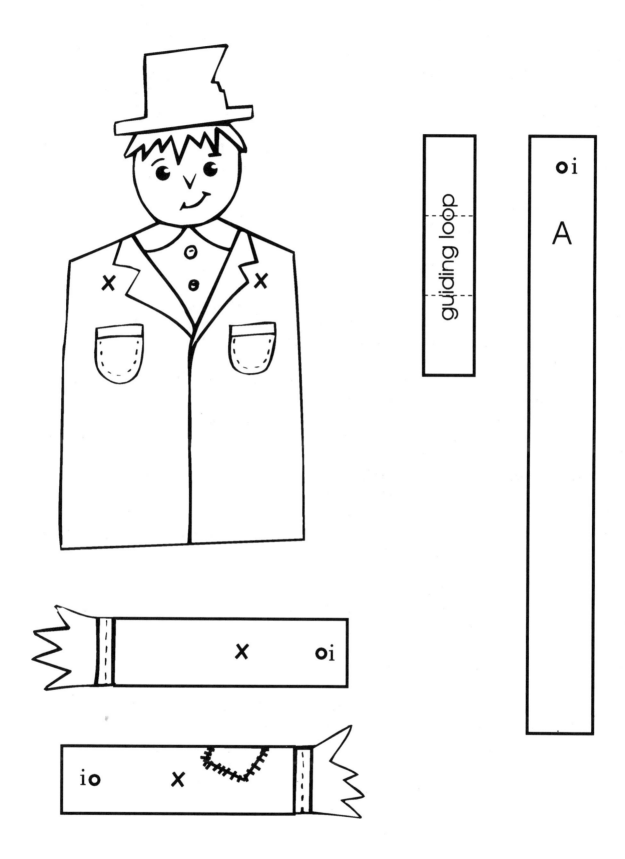

Moving Tortoise Card

Technique Used:

Multiple T Shaped Levers

Equipment needed:

scissors
card
felt pens
6 brass fasteners
hole punch or paper drill

How to make the example:

Step 1. Photocopy the sheet opposite onto card or paste onto card.
Step 2. Cut out the legs, head, tail and body shapes and make small holes with a pointed pair of scissors over the small circles marked on the pieces.
Step 3. Colour in all the tortoise pieces.
Step 4. Fasten the head and the tail to E with either brass fasteners [or eyelets] at i. (remember to make holes first).
Step 4. Fasten the front leg [F] and the back leg [B] to E as marked at ii.
Step 5. Make holes through the X marks on the legs, head and tail and in the tortoise body at S,T,U and V.
Step 6. Fasten the head, tail and legs to the body with brass fasteners or eyelets.
By pushing and pulling the centre strip E, the head tail and legs of the tortoise will move upwards and downwards.
The end product may be mounted on the inside or outside of a greetings card and a suitable message added.

Head, tail and legs = Levers
S, T, U, V = Fixed points/fulcra (one = fulcrum)
E = effort to move them.

How the idea may be developed:

This introduces the technique; now the pupils must experiment to make a creature/ person with moving limbs. Teacher made and manufactured items will help in the pupils' designing.

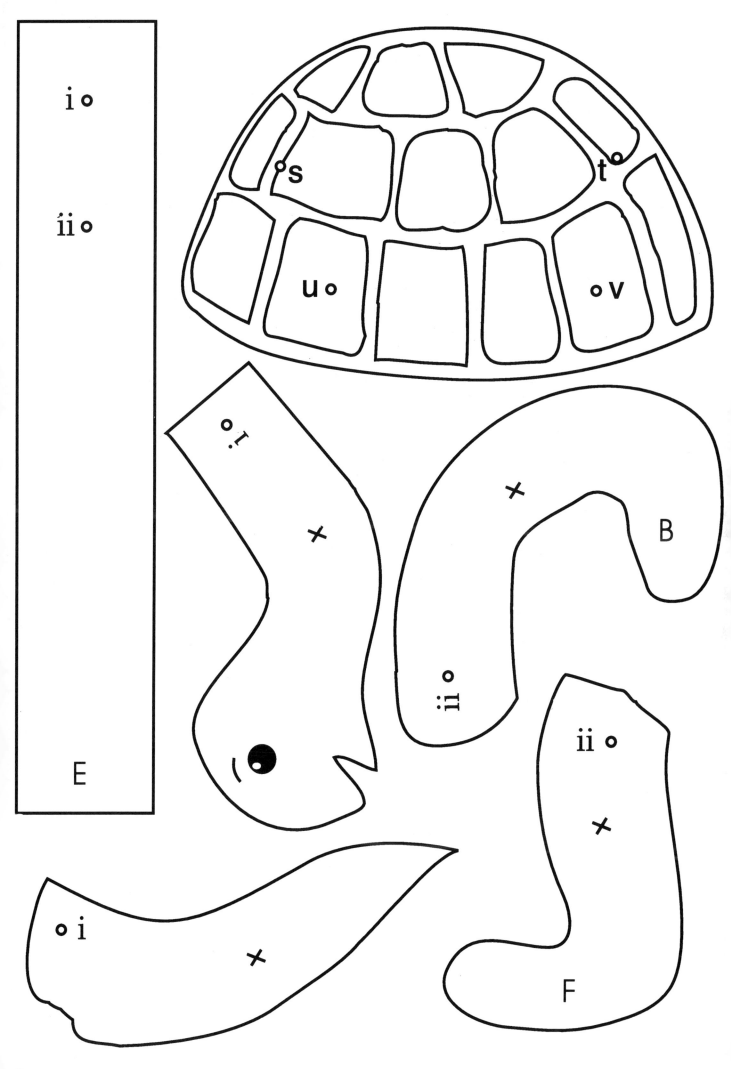

Fiery Dragon Card

Technique used:

Linkages

Equipment needed:

scissors
2 brass fasteners
glue
felt pens, crayons

How to make the Example:

Step 1. Photocopy the sheet opposite onto card, one per child, or make templates to draw around.
Step 2. Cut out the pieces and decorate.
Step 3. Fasten A to the tongue with a brass fastener at i.
Step 4. Fasten A to the back of the card through the X's as indicated.
Step 5. Make the guiding loop by folding the strip of card along the dotted lines and glueing the third section in place.
Step 6. Thread the guiding loop over the tongue and glue into place on the reverse side of the Dragons head, behind the position marked with the dotted outline.
Step 7. By moving A left and right the dragons tongue will stick in and out.
Step 8. Attach a loop made out of ribbon, card or wool to the top of the card to enable it to be hung for displaying as in the diagram.

How the idea may be developed:

The linkages can be used the other way up to create objects that will pop up and down. A slot can be placed in the background and the strip threaded through to the front of the pupil's design.

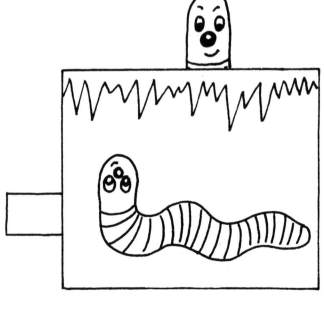

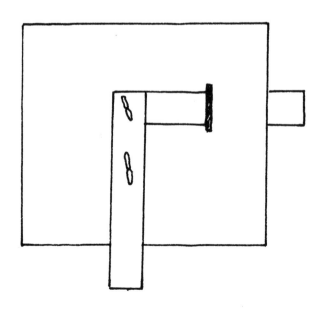

oi

A

tongue io

Moving Ostrich Card

Technique Used:

Z Shaped Linkage

Equipment needed:

scissors
thick card
3 brass fasteners
felt pens, wax or coloured pencil crayons
hole punch or paper drill
glue
one sheet of A4 card

How to make the example:

Step 1. Photocopy the sheet opposite and paste onto thick card, one per child.
Step 2. Cut out the ostrich head, neck, body and legs.
Step 3. Colour in the ostrich pieces.
Step 4. Make small holes with the pointed end of a pair of scissors through the small circles on all the ostrich pieces
Step 5. Fasten the head to the neck through the holes at i.
Step 6. Fasten the neck to the body through the holes at ii.
Step 7. Fasten the neck to the front of a folded piece of A4 card at X as in the diagram above to create your greetings card.
Step 8. Cut a slot in the A4 piece of card and thread the tab through the slot as above.

How the idea may be developed:

Let the pupils experiment with this linkage using strips of card and fasteners.
Children can investigate what happens when the tabs are pushed and pulled. Would guiding loops help them move? Can the mechanism be used the other way up? Pupils can use this mechanism to create their own moving creatures?

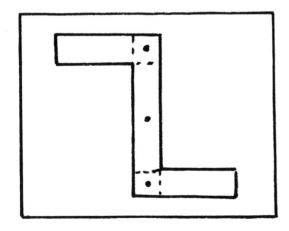
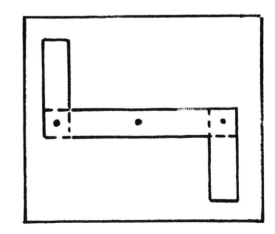

56

Pecking Bird Card

Technique Used:

Parallel Linkages

Equipment needed:

thick card
glue
scissors
4 brass fasteners
coloured pencils or felt pens

How to make the example:

Step 1. Photocopy the sheet opposite and paste onto thick card.
Step 2. Cut out the strips A, B, C & D and cut out the bowl of bird food and the two birds.
Step 3. Decorate the birds and the bowl of food.
Step 4. Position C over A and fasten together through the small circles at ii with a brass fastener (remember to make holes first).
Step 5. Position C over B and fasten together through the holes at i with a brass fastener.
Step 6. Position D over A and fasten together at the holes marked at i.
Step 7. Position D over B and fasten together at the holes marked at ii.
Step 8. Glue the birds and food bowl in position as above.

How the idea may be developed:

Talk to the children about what happens when X is pushed or pulled.
Pupils could make this mechanism out of strips of wood.

oii   A   oi

oi   B   oii

oii   C   oi

oi   D   oii

Moving Circus Card

Technique Used:
>   Straight Line Slot.

Equipment needed
>   scissors
>   craft knife
>   safety ruler
>   cutting mat
>   glue sticks
>   felt pens and crayons

How to make the example:

Step 1. Photocpy the sheet opposite onto card or stick onto card, one per child.

Step 2. Cut out A and with a craft knife, safety ruler and cutting mat the teacher should show the pupils how the slot is cut out.
Take care to emphasise the safety aspects of using a craft knife.

Step 3. C and D are guiding loops. They should be cut out and folded along the dotted lines to make a loop.
These loops are then positioned on the reverse side of the card, at each end of the slot, the top of the guiding loop level with the slot.
Glue the guiding loops in place.

Step 4. Cut out the control rod B, and stick it onto thicker card. The control rod fits through the loops and the tab goes through the slot.

Step 5. Attach stop ends to the control rod and the clown to the tab. By pulling and pushing the control rod, movement in a straight line is obtained.

How the idea may be developed.

The slot can be horizontal, vertical or diagonal. Pictures to stick onto the tab can be created by the pupils or cut out of old greetings cards etc.

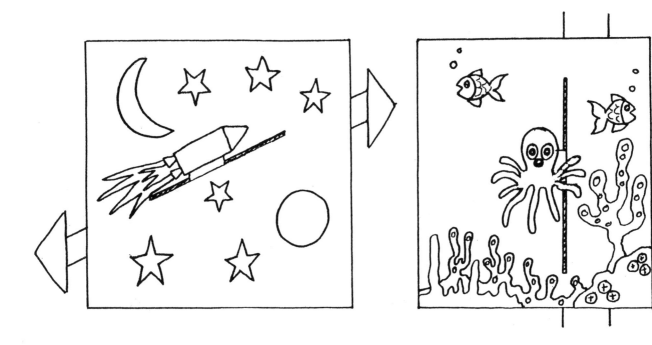

C

D

Tab

B

CIRCUS FUN

A

Happy Birthday

Moving Star Card

Technique used:

Circular Motion

Equipment used:

scissors
cutting mat
craft knife or compass cutter
2 brass fasteners
felt pens, wax crayons or coloured pencils
glue stick
hole punch or paper drill

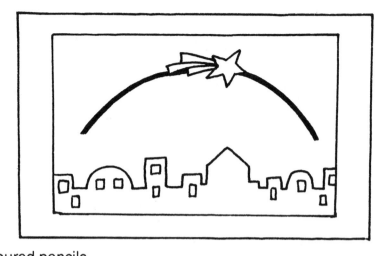

How to make the example:

Step 1. Photocopy the sheet opposite and the pieces below onto card or stick onto card, one per child.

Step 2. Cut out the pieces and decorate. The teacher must supervise very carefully as individual pupils cut out the curved slot using a craft knife or compass cutter and cutting mat.

Step 3. Glue strips A and B onto thicker card.

Step 4. Attach A to B at i with a brass fastener or an eyelet.

Step 5. Thread A through the cut slot and attach it to the background with a brass fastener through the x's. Make sure strips A and B move freely.

Step 6. Make the guiding loop and thread it over B. Attach it to the background.

Step 7. By pulling and pushing B, the rod a will move in an arc.

Step 8. Attach the star to the tab A and watch the star move over Bethlehem.

Step 9. Attach a piece of ribbon, card or string to the top of the picture as in the above diagram to create a hanging greetings card. The message can be written on the reverse side or attached to a small tag hanging from the bottom of the picture.

How the idea may be developed:

The pupils should be given the time to create their own picture with a moving part.

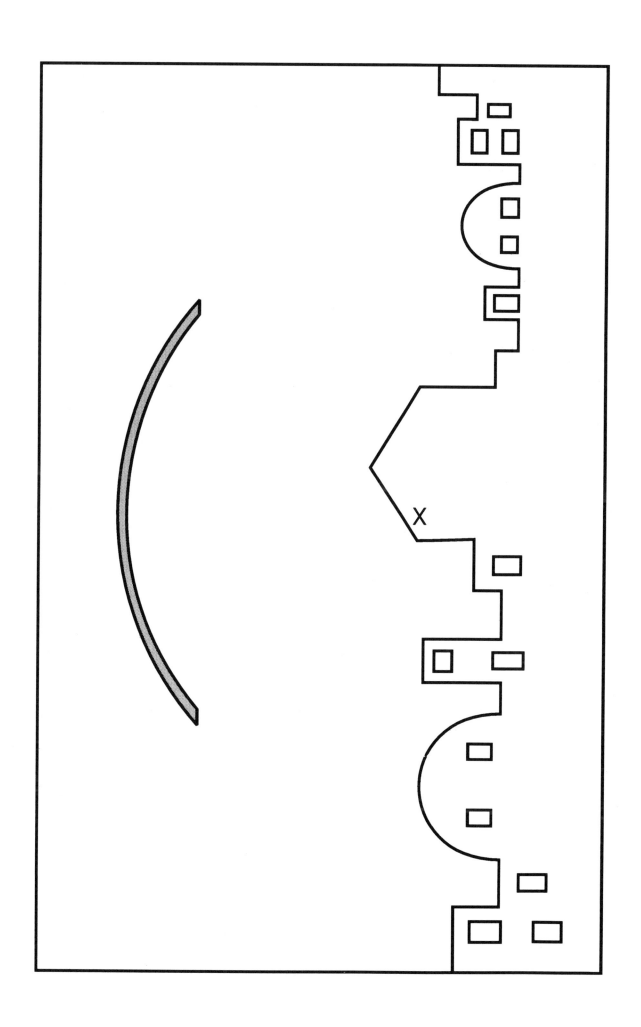

Let's Experiment

Technique used:

Linkages

Equipment needed:

scissors or utility snips
4 brass fasteners
A4 card
thick card
glue

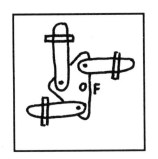
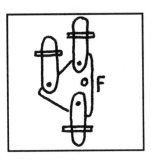
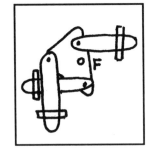
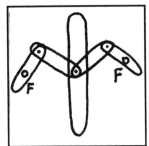

Can the pupils make these examples?

How to make the examples:

Step 1. Photocopy the shapes below, cut them out and and stick onto thick card. Use as templates.

Step 2. Without teacher intervention as the pupils will already have been introduced to the joining techniques, let the pupils cut out the necessary shapes to create the examples shown.

Step 3. The pupils should be given time to experiment with the direction of movement when the different strips are pushed and pulled

How the idea can be developed:

How can the pupils record their investigations?
Can they use these linkages to create 'something'?
Can other materials be used?

Use these pieces as templates

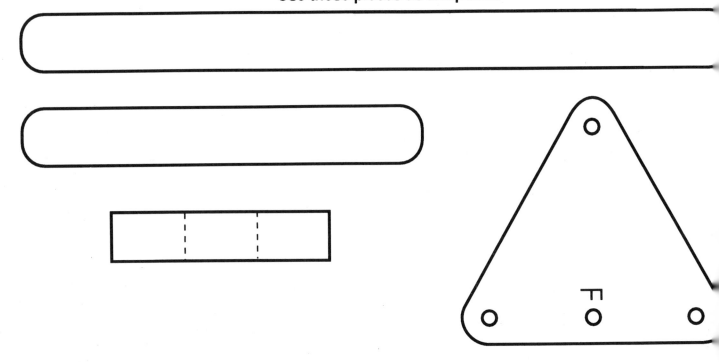